MOTIVATION

READ ME DAILY

All You Need To Supercharge Your Day And Light the Fire Within

Russell Duncan

Table of Contents

Chapter 1: Why You Need To Find Your Why 6
Chapter 2: *Your Motivational Partner In Life* 9
Chapter 3: Why You Are Setting The Wrong Goals 12
Chapter 4: Twenty Percent of Effort Produces 80% of Results 15
Chapter 5: Your Mind is A Suggestion Engine 18
Chapter 6: This Is Life 21
Chapter 7: *Stop Ignoring Your Health* 24
Chapter 8: Stay Focused 27
Chapter 9: There's No Time for Regrets 32
Chapter 10: Share Your Troubles Freely and Openly 36
Chapter 11: *How to Build Skills That Are Valuable* 39
Chapter 12: How To Win The Most Attention From Others 42
Chapter 13: How To Rid Yourself of Distraction 45
Chapter 14: How Much Is Your Time Really Worth? 49
Chapter 15: Be Inspired to Create 51
Chapter 16: When To Listen To That Voice Inside Your Head 53
Chapter 17: Overcoming the Fear of Failure 56
Chapter 18: How To Deal With Uncertainty? 59
Chapter 19: The Only Obstacle Is Yourself 63
Chapter 20: 7 Ways To Know If You're A Good Person 67
Chapter 21: Do More of What Already Works 72
Chapter 22: Becoming High Achievers 75
Chapter 23: Overcoming Fear and Self-Doubt 80
Chapter 24: Get in the Water (Stop wasting time) 83
Chapter 25: Creating Successful Habits 85
Chapter 26: Focus On The Work You Need To Do Today 90
Chapter 27: It's Okay To Feel Uncertain 93
Chapter 28: When It's Okay to Do Nothing 96

Chapter 29: *Be Motivated by Challenge* 100

Chapter 30: Don't Fear Judgement 103

Chapter 31: Discovering Your Strengths and Weaknesses 106

Chapter 32: *Don't Be Demotivated By Fear* 109

Chapter 33: Deal With Your Fears Now 112

Chapter 34: Never Giving Up 116

Chapter 35: Keep Moving When Things Get Hard 119

Chapter 36: How To Succeed In Life 123

Chapter 37: Being Mentally Strong 127

Chapter 1:
Why You Need To Find Your Why

Your why is your reason for being.
Your reason for living.
Your reason for acting.
Without a why life begins to feel demoralising.
Without a purpose, what is the purpose?
What chance do you think you have of achieving anything, without a reason?

Go out and ask 20 people why they are working, apart from the pay.
Roughly 16 will not be able to give you a clear answer, and 4 will.
The 4 that will have a plan and a goal to achieve more.
They probably already are more successful than the 16 with no answer.

The 4 know their current work is just a step to a bigger goal.
They know their what and their why behind everything they are doing.

The 16 just landed in that job by chance and will probably never leave it.
They may progress up the company ladder slowly,
But with no clear reason to achieve anything greater they will stay where they are, in perceived security.

Do you know why you are doing what you are doing?

If not, it's about time you discover your why.

It may be to providing a better life for your family and friends.

Your motives may be financial, they may not.

Maybe your why is to lead a less stressful life.

Maybe that means your require less money to be happy.

Your reason is individual and personal.

No one else should influence that.

Seek to heed advice from people who are where you want to be in life.

You wouldn't let a mechanic perform surgery on you,

so why would you accept advice on success from the unsuccessful.

They may be successful in their field.

But if their field is not your field, they have no business telling you how to play.

Their why is not your why, and their what is not your what.

If the goals and reasons are different, the advice is irrelevant.

Politely respect their advice.

Use their success to fuel your drive for success in your own field.

Help it guide you to a similar path that you are aiming towards.

Your why is so important.

It will be the reason you persist when things get tough.

If you have no clearly defined reason, it becomes easy for you to quit.

A clearly defined goal (your what),

and a clearly defined reason (your why),

are critical to any lasting happiness and success.

Without them you are just aimlessly drifting from nothing to nothing.

Without clearly defining the terms of your life , you forfeit the power of your will and your life will be decided by someone else.

That is tragedy.

Your why truly is everything on the path to achieving your what.

Your end goal.

Your dream life.

Everything that you will sit down and clearly define.

The detail of everything and the people who will enjoy it - your ultimate why.

What and why go together like salt and pepper or bread and butter.

You can't have one without the other.

Chapter 2:

<u>Your Motivational Partner In Life</u>

We all have friends. We all have parents. We may have a partner or other half. We all have teachers.

We love and respect all of them and hopefully, they do too. But have we ever wondered why we do that?

Why do we have to love someone who brought us into this world? Why do we love a person who is not related to us whatsoever, but has a connection with us, and hence we like to hang around them? Why do we respect someone who is being paid to do what makes him respectable?

The answer to all these is simple. They make us a better version of ourselves. Without these people in our lives, we won't be as good as we are right now.

It doesn't matter where we stand right now in our lives, there would always be someone backing you up whenever you feel low.

People tend to seek loneliness and a quiet corner whenever life hits hard. But what they don't realize is that there are people in their lives who have a duty towards you.

Either that be your parents or friends or partner or anyone for that case, you need to find time to give them a chance to show their true affections towards you. You need to give them

Your parents can't give up on you because you are a part of them. You have their legacy to keep and spread. They want you to be a better person than they ever were, hence they will always support you no matter what the world does to you.

Your friends have a bond of loyalty towards you which is the basic root of any friendship. They will always try to help you get up no matter how many times you fall.

All these people owe you this support. And you owe it to them to be a source of inspiration when they want a shoulder to cry. When they want a person to listen and feel their pain. When they need someone to be able to share some time with them without a grain of self-interest.

These things make us stronger as a human and make us grow and evolve as a Specie.

You can find motivation and inspiration from anyone. It may even be a guard in your office or a worker in your office who you might see once a week.

Basic human nature makes us susceptible to the need of finding company. It doesn't matter where it comes from. What you need is a person who can devote a selfless minute of his or her life to you and feels good when they realize they have made a positive change in your life.

Everyone goes through this phase of loneliness but we always find a person who makes us the most comfortable.

The person who reimburses our self-belief. The person who makes us take one more try, one more chance, not for us but for them too. This person is your true motivational partner in life.

Chapter 3:
Why You Are Setting The Wrong Goals

Ever wondered why you are not getting any closer to your goals? Why you keep failing despite having all that effort? Why does someone else seem to be more successful?

Here are some thoughts for you to ponder.

You may have a good set of skills and all the eligibility criteria anyone else has. But you are not yet in the same spot you wished some years ago. Maybe it is not happening for your right now, because your approach to those goals is not correct. Or, maybe your goals are wrong altogether.

Let's say you had a goal to be someone or achieve something someday. But you never had any idea how to! So you started asking why am I not getting the success that I deserve, but never asked yourself, how can I get to that success.

So you might think that you have the right goals to achieve something. But the reality is, that you never had the right goals.

You should have set a single goal a single day. A single goal that you can achieve in a day will help you get on the right train at the right time with a limited effort.

You shouldn't think of the future itself, but the goal that you might achieve someday. Once you have that goal in mind, you shouldn't need a constant reminder every day just to create a scenario of depression and restlessness that won't help you rather strain unnecessary energy.

Once you have the final goal, put it aside and work towards the small goals that you can achieve in real-time with actual small efforts.

Once you have a grasp of these goals, you will find the next goal yourself; a goal that you might have never thought of before.

Just say you want to lose weight and you want to get to your ideal BMI someday. This is a valid and reasonable Goal to achieve. This might prolong your life and increase your self-worth. So you should have a set of regular goals that ultimately lead you to the final goal.

So you want to lose weight, start by reducing fats and carbs in your next meal, and the one after that and the next one.

It will be hard the first time. Maybe the same at the second time. But when you have envisioned the ultimate goal, you will be content with the healthier alternates as well.

Add 5 minutes of exercise the next day, along with the goals of the previous day. You will be reluctant to do it the first time, but when you see the sweat dripping from your chin, you will see your healthier self in each drop.

Every goal has its process. No matter how much you avoid the process, you will always find yourself at the mercy of mother nature, and nature has always a plan for execution.

Now it's your decision whether to be a part of that process or go down in history with a blank face with no name.

You will always find a way to cheat, but to cheat is another ten steps away from your penultimate goal.

Make it your goal to resist every temptation that makes your day no different than the previous one. Live your life on One day, Monday, Change day principle and you will always find yourself closer to your salvation.

The process of change is mundane. In fact, the process of everything in life is mundane. You have to apply certain steps and procedures for even doing the most basic tasks in your daily life.

Stop procrastinating because you are not fooling anyone else, just yourself. And if you keep fooling yourself, you will be the worst failure in the books of history.

Chapter 4:
Twenty Percent of Effort Produces 80% of Results

Today we're going to talk about the 80-20 rule and how you can apply it to your life for great results in whatever you are doing. For the purposes of this video we are going to use income as a measurement of success. This will directly translate to productivity and the areas that you are spending your most time and energy.

Have you ever wondered why no matter how much time you end up working, that your paycheck never seems to rise? That your income and finance seems to be stagnant? Or have you ever wondered, for those of you who have ventured into creating a second or third stream of income on the side, that you might actually spend lesser on those activities and earn a bigger income in proportion to the time you actually spent to run those side businesses?

This is where the 80-20 rule comes into play. For those that have not seen their bank account or income grow despite the immense amount of effort put it, It may be that 80% of time you are spending it doing things that actually have little or no change to the growth of your networth. The work simply isn't actually worth 80% of your attention.

Rather you may want to look elsewhere, to that 20%, if you want to see real change. I would recommend that instead of banging your head against the wall at your day job, try looking for something to do on the side. It may be just your passion, or it may be something you foresee greater potential returns. Start taking action on those things. It could be the very thing that you were searching for this whole time. If the rule applies, you should be spending majority of your time and energy into this 20%. By focusing on the tasks that has the greatest rewards, you are working smart instead of working hard now. Only when you can identify what exactly those tasks are can you double down on them for great success.

There were times in my life that I spent a lot of my time trying to force something to work. But no matter how hard I tried, I just couldn't see a breakthrough. It was only after further exploration through trials and errors did I finally come up with a set list of tasks that I knew were profitable. That if I kept doing them over and over again I would be able to grow my wealth consistently. By spending all of my time doing these specific tasks, I was able to eliminate all the noise and to focus my actions to a narrow few. And I was surprised at the outsized rewards it brought me.

If you know that something isn't working, don't be afraid to keep looking, trying, and exploring other ways. Keep a close tab on the time you spend in these areas and the income that flows in. Only when you measure everything can you really know where you are going wrong and where you are going right.

Remember that 20% of the effort produces 80% of the results. So I challenge all of you to stop spending 80% of the effort doing things that only produce 20% of the results. It is better to work smart than to work hard. Trust me. I believe that you will be able to find what those things are if you put your mind to it.

Chapter 5:
Your Mind is A Suggestion Engine

What we go through each day and what we want every day is what our mind wants us to think and believe.

Let's just think about, whatever you are doing right now apart from reading this post. Something your mind came up with by making a reasonable argument with you.

So what you have in your mind right now, is your reality. You have memories of your past that are related to actual people and places that you have encountered or been to in your life.

So you go in that place of your mind where you have to be in charge of what to feel right now. But it's not you who wants to be in charge, it's your brain that is the one dictating you.

It's not wrong to say that your conscious mind is your master. The mind is the master of the body.

If at any time in your life you feel lost and have a breakdown, where you don't have a solution for your current problems, just pause for a moment. Give your mind some time to try out new things and it will certainly push you new ideas.

There is no feasible problem that you cannot solve. You only need to give the problem and your mind some time to familiarize and you will surely get the best possible solution and the easiest way out.

If at any time you decide to pull out, just stay put and give your mind a moment. It will make you visualize the things you will miss out on and the things that you wouldn't be able to achieve if you don't go after them.

Your life is the sum total of all your positive and negative thoughts. If you keep having negative thoughts it means you have equipped your mind with things that you shouldn't have. It means that you are not giving your mind enough space to generate newer and better thoughts and ideas for you to work on.

The harder you concentrate on your failures, the more chance you have to get stuck. Stuck in a place where neither your brain nor your body is teaming up with your fate.

So you have to be cautious of what you want to believe in and what you want to pursue in your leisure time. Because if you cannot control that suggestion engine on top, then you would surely have a dismal life and it won't be anyone else's fault.

If you want a day full of happy thoughts and feelings, you have to try to replace any negative thought that comes up in your mind with not one but two happy thoughts.

You yourself have to create your own reality that you live in. For that, you have to train your mind. Train it in such a way that you can generate an array of wild yet soothing, comforting, and loving thoughts. That promotes you to go the extra mile and live like a whole and a new Human Being.

You can do anything, just till you keep facing your fears and having an acceptance of them.

Chapter 6:

This Is Life

Who doesn't ponder the most basic and primary question, 'What is Life?' It is a bit cliche, but not unnecessary at all. And it certainly isn't illogical to think about what we are and what we have.

We often take life for granted but never realize what we have is special. We never contemplate the most important aspect of our existence.

We evolve during our time on this Earth. We start from nothing. But build towards a stronger being with greater and much better ambitions. We try to excel at everything we cross paths with. We strive towards our conscious development. We work towards our physical as well as emotional well-being.

We have a lot to live for but we rarely try to live for what matters the most. We never try to live like we have a greater purpose. Rather we try to go for petty things that might not even last for that long.

Life is short compared to what is going on around us. But we have to live it like there are unlimited seasons to come, each with its own blessings, each with its own opportunities.

We, humans, have evolved enough to be able to see beyond most plain things, but we chose to get soaked up in shallow waters. This life is a deep ocean with limits practically unpredictable.

Life is unexpected, it's unintentional, it's fussy but worth living for.

The life we see today is the collection of infinite, unbroken, and eternal events, rippling together simultaneously.

We say someone is alive when we see them breathing and moving but we never really know if that person is actually alive inside. We never really think about if the person is happy inside and enjoying what they have right now. We never try to look through the person and help them be alive for what matters.

Life never treats everyone the same way. But you don't need to get depressed every time you miss an alarm, or perform badly in an exam, or don't have the proper stats to show for your annual sales.

It doesn't always end badly and it certainly isn't bad every time of every day. It's just our psychology that makes us treat ourselves and life in a way that makes life demeaning and not worth it.

Everything is worth it once you try to look past the bad things and focus on the good ones you still get left with.

You have this one life, so go and live it like it matters the most to you. You might have to get a bit selfish and you might have to offend some people. Not deliberately, but just because you need some time and space which they might not allow, but it doesn't matter.

The epitome of life is that you have a clock ticking with each second getting you closer to the end. But you can still run around the clock and make it work as a swing. Enjoy with a purpose. Lead with your heart and you will come across wonders.

Chapter 7:
<u>Stop Ignoring Your Health</u>

Do you have a busy life? Do you follow a hard and continuous regime of tasks every day for a significant amount of time? Have you ever felt that you cannot enjoy even the happiest moments of your life even if you want to? Let me highlight one reason you might recognize it straight away.

You are not enjoying your days while still being in all your senses because you don't have your mind and body in the right place.

All these years you have lived your life as a race. You have taken part in every event in and around your life just because you never wanted to miss anything. But in this process, you never lived your life to its full potential. You never lived a single moment with just the emotional intention of being then and there and not trying to live it like just another day or event.

People often get so busy with making their careers that they don't realize what is more important in life? It is their mental and physical health!

You will not get anywhere far in your life if you keep ignoring the signs of sickness your body keeps giving you. Your body is a machine with a conditional warranty. The day you violate the conditions of this warranty, life will become challenging and you won't even be interested in the basic tasks at hand.

You might have heard the famous saying that "Health is Wealth". Let it sink in for a while and analyze your own life. You don't need to be a top-tier athlete to have a good body. You need a good body for your organs to work properly. You need an active lifestyle to be more productive and be more present and engaged in the things that are going around you.

The dilemma of our lives is that we don't care about what we have right now, but we care a lot about what we want. Not realizing that what we want might be cursed but what we have is the soul of good living. And that my friends are the blessing of health that most of us take for granted.

Most people have a tendency and devotion to work specifically on their health and fitness on a priority basis. They have a better standard of life. These people have a clearer mind to feel and capture the best moments in life with what their senses can offer best to them.

If you don't stop ignoring your health, you won't ever get out of this constant struggle. The struggle to find the reasons for you being detached from everything despite being involved every time.

Being careful and observant of your health doesn't make you selfish. This makes you a much more caring person because not only your life but the life of others around you is also affected by your sickness. Not only your resources are used for your treatments but the attention and emotions of your loved ones are also being spent, just in hope of your wellness.

Chapter 8:

Stay Focused

A razor sharp focus is required to bridge the gap
between our vision and our current circumstances.
Stay focused on the vision we want,
despite the current reality.
It's challenging to believe you will be rich when you are poor,
healthy if you are sick,
but it is necessary to achieve that vision.

Focus on the desired result.
Focus on the next step towards that goal.
Without focus on these elements there can be no success.
Stay focused on the positive elements,
solutions over problems.

The expected reward over the fear, loss and pain along the way.
What we focus on will become.
Therefore we have to maintain our eyes on the prize.

Be results driven.
Always focus on bringing that result closer.
Focus on what your grateful for.
Gratefulness brings more of that into your life.

Focus on problems on the other hand brings more problems.

If we focus on a big goal today,
we might not be ready yet,
but we will become ready on the way.

Commit to the necessary changes you know you need.
Get ourselves ready for that goal.
So many never act simply because they don't know how.
They don't feel ready.
We can achieve nearly anything if we focus on it.

Think carefully about what you focus on.
It is critical to both your success and failure.
Know exactly what you want.
See the odds of a successful happy life increase by unfathomable amounts.

How can we be happy and successful if we never define what that is?
It's not about what you are, or what you were in the past.
It is all about what you are becoming and want to become.

We cannot let circumstances or the world decide that.
We must use our free will and decide who and what we will become and focus fully on that.
Wishing, succumbing to the days whim, will never bring lasting success.
Success requires serious commitment and focus on that outcome.

Exude a fanatical level of focus.

Be exuberated in the pursuit of success.

The most successful often focus on work for over 100 hours per week.

They give up most social interaction and even sleep to make that dream happen.

They do not find this hard or stressful because they are pursuing something they enjoy.

Focus on something you enjoy.

Stop spending your time and energy on a job that you hate.

Work in an area you enjoy.

It makes focusing and achieving success easier.

Keep in mind that your time is limited.

Is what you're doing right now moving you towards your goal?

If not stop.

It is crucial that you enjoy your journey.

Start planning some leisure time into your days.

The goal is to remain balanced while you stick to your schedule.

If you focus on nothing, you will receive nothing.

If you do nothing, you will become nothing.

Your focus is everything.

Get specific with your focus to steer your ships in the direction of the solid fertile land you desire.
Aim higher as you focus on bigger and better things.

Why focus on plan b if you believe in plan a?
Why not give all your focus to that?

Stay focused on the best result regardless of the perceived situation.
The world is pliable.
It will mould and change around you based on your thoughts and what you focus on.
Your free will means you are free to focus on what you want and ignore what you don't.

Focus on a future of greatness.
A future where you are healthy, happy, and wealthy.
See the limits as imaginary and watch them break down before you.
Understand that you are powerful and what you think matters in your life.

Become who you want to be,
Not who others think you should be.
This shift is one of the quickest roads to happiness.

When you focus on what you love,
You draw more of it into our lives.
You will become happier.

You must focus on a future that makes you and your family happy.

You must stay steadfast with an unwavering faith and focus on that result.

Because with faith and focus anything is possible.

Chapter 9:
There's No Time for Regrets

Regret. Guilt. Shame.

These are three of the darkest emotions any human will ever experience. We all feel these things at different points in our lives, especially after making a "bad" decision. There are certain situations some of us would rewind (or delete) if we could. The reality is, however, there is an infinite number of reasons we should never regret any of the decisions we make in our lives.

Here are 7 of them:

1. Every decision allows you to take credit for creating your own life.

Decisions are not always the result of thoughtful contemplation. Some of them are made on impulse alone. Regardless of the decision, when you made it, it was something you wanted, or you would not have done it (unless someone was pointing a gun at your head).

Be willing to own the decisions you make. Be accountable for them. Take responsibility and accept them.

2. By making any decision involving your heart, you have the chance to create more love in the world by spreading yours.

Your love is a gift.

Once you decide to love, do it without reservation. By fully giving of yourself, you expand your ability to express and receive love. You have added to the goodness of our universe by revealing your heart to it.

3. By experiencing the disappointment that might come with a decision's outcome, you can propel yourself to a new level of emotional evolution.

You aren't doing yourself any favors when you try to save yourself from disappointment. Disappointment provides you with an opportunity to redefine your experiences in life. By refining your reframing skills, you increase your resilience.

4. "Bad" decisions are your opportunity to master the art of self-forgiveness.

When you make a "bad" decision, *you* are the person who is usually the hardest on yourself. Before you can accept the consequences of your decision and move on, you must forgive yourself. You won't always make perfect choices in your life. Acknowledge the beauty in your human imperfection, then move forward and on.

5. Because of the occasional misstep, you enable yourself to live a Technicolor life.

Anger. Joy. Sadness.

These emotions add pigment to your life. Without these things, you would feel soulless. Your life would be black and white.

Make your decisions with gusto. Breathe with fire. You are here to live in color.

6. Your ability to make a decision is an opportunity to exercise the freedom that is your birthright.

How would you feel if you had no say in those decisions concerning your life? Would you feel powerless? Restricted? Suffocated?

Now, focus on what it feels like to make the decisions you want to make. What do you feel? Freedom? Liberty? Independence?

What feelings do you *want* to feel?

Freedom. Liberty. Independence.

As luck would have it, the freedom you want is yours. Be thankful for it in every decision you make, "good" or "bad."

7. When you decide to result in ugly aftermath, you refine what you *do* want in your life.

It's often impossible to know what you want until you experience what you don't want. With every decision, you will experience consequences.

Use those outcomes as a jumping-off point to something different (and better) in your future.

Chapter 10:
Share Your Troubles Freely and Openly

Life is hard. We go through tons of challenges, problems, and obstacles every single day. We accumulate problems and stresses left right and Center. Absorbing each impact blow for blow.

Over time, these impacts will wear us down mentally and physically. Without a proper release channel, we find that our emotions spill over in ways when we least expect it. We get easily irritated, have a hard time falling asleep, have mood issues, and find ourselves even being temporarily depressed at times.

When we bottle negativity, it festers inside us without us realising what we have done. That is where releasing those tensions by pouring our heart and soul into friends, writing, journaling, and other outlets that allow us to express our feelings freely without judgement.

We may not all have friends that we can truly count on to share our deepest darkest secrets for fear that they might share these secrets unsuspectingly. If we do have these types of friends, treasure them and seek them out regularly to share your problems. By bouncing ideas off someone, we may even find a new solution to an old problem that we couldn't before. The other party may also be able to see things more objectively and with a unique perspective that is contrary to yours which you could potentially use to your advantage.

If writing things down is something that helps you cope with life, then by all means take a piece of paper and write down all the things that have been bothering you. Journal it, archive it. You may even write a song about it if that helps you process things better. Writing things down help us clear our minds and lets us see the big picture when we come back to it at a later date should we feel ready to address it. When things are too crazy, we may not have the mental capacity to handle everything being thrown at us at one go. So take the time to sort those feelings out.

You may also choose to just find a place that brings you relaxation. Whether it be going to the beach, or renting a hotel, or even just screaming at the top of your lungs. Let those feelings out. Don't keep it hidden inside.

IF all these things still don't work for you, you may want to try seeking help from a professional counsellor or therapist who can work out these issues you have in your life one by one. Never be afraid to book an appointment because your mental health is more important than the stigma associated with seeing a professional. You are not admitting you have a problem, you are simply acknowledge that there are areas in your life that you need assistance with. And that it is perfectly okay and perfectly normal to do so. Counsellors have the passion to serve, the passion to help, and that is why they chose that profession to being with. So seek their assistance and guidance as much as you need to.

Life isn't easy. But we can all take a conscious effort to regulate our emotions more healthily to live a long and balanced life.

Chapter 11:

How to Build Skills That Are Valuable

The most valuable skills you can have in life and work are rarely taught in school, never show up on a resume, and are consistently overlooked and underappreciated. But there's some good news: It costs nothing to develop them, and you have the opportunity to do so.

Here's how

1. The Ability To Pay Attention

The shorter the average attention span gets, the more valuable your ability to focus becomes.

It's a huge competitive advantage to be able to pay attention to things for an extended period (and unfortunately, what passes for an extended period these days may be as little as 10 minutes).

The ability to pay attention helps you learn, communicate, be productive, and see opportunities others miss, among countless other things.

Two ways to improve your ability to pay attention:

- Practice single-tasking — read a book, watch a movie, or find some other thing to do for an extensive amount of time without allowing yourself to do anything else during that time. No side conversations. No checking your phone. Nothing but focus on that one thing.

- Become intentional with how you use your phone (and for the love of God, turn off your notifications!).

2. The Ability To Follow Directions

This one takes your improved ability to pay attention a step further.

Every aspect of your life and career involves directions —customers tell you what they want, your boss tells you what she needs to be done, and the people you care about tell you what they expect of you.

It's one thing to pay attention to instructions, but it's another to accurately follow them.

The best qualifications in the world won't land you a job if your application doesn't include the employer's requested details.

Your company won't care about your innovative ideas if they don't align with the problems they asked you to solve.

And the reason Facebook Ads may not work for you isn't that Facebook ads don't work — it's because you don't know the right ways to use them. The ability to follow directions serves as a filter that keeps otherwise qualified people from succeeding — and most of them don't even realize their struggles are rooted in this weakness.

Don't let that be you.

Two ways to improve your ability to follow directions:

1. Ask for directions on how to do things more often. Practice makes perfect.
2. Give directions to other people. Take something you know how to do (like write a blog post, for example), and write up directions to help others do it the way you do (like I did here). Teaching is a great

way to learn, and the process of creating directions will help you recognize the importance of little steps in directions you get from others.

The point of this post isn't to make you feel overwhelmed. The truth is, you already have these skills — we all do. But I wrote this because I've noticed many people don't think about these abilities as skills and therefore don't do much to hone them.

Chapter 12:
How To Win The Most Attention From Others

Attention. If you only knew how much power attention over someone actually holds. You see, to achieve fame, success, and power, you need to master how to grab someone's attention and never let it go.

The Biggest companies in the world have become so good at this that they are able to hold a command over their most loyal followers by capturing their time and energy into using their products and services. We unknowingly give our time and energy to these great companies because they have mastered the art of taking our attention and never letting go of it. Think of Apple, when they launch a new product, be it an iPhone, ipad, or whatever software and services, almost all the attention and media coverage goes to them. And everyone pays "attention" to what they have to do or say because they hold such an enormous power in the tech industry.

When Princess Diana first graced us in the 1980s, many of us who were still not alive back then, she grabbed the world by storm by always being the Center of attention in all media and news outlets. She had the world in the palm of her hands. The world wanted more of her and all of their attention is spent on watching and analysing her every move. She was the most famous person on Earth for many years right up until her untimely death in 1997.

Fortunately for Princess Diana, she knew how to use the attention while she was alive to good use. She advocated for many humanitarian causes that shed light on issues such as AIDS, landmines, and many issues that were big taboos back then. Whichever causes she dedicated her time to, they benefited from her star power and presence and she lifted many of the stigma associated with it and also helped raise funds for them.

From these two simple examples we now understand how much power attention wields. When you have someone's attention, whether it be 1 person or 1 billion people, you have a hold over them and they will be watching you.

This is why many social media companies are all fighting to get your attention, whether it be through views or paid posts, they want you to be spending time on their platform so that you can spend money with them. That is how they earn their billions from everyone's collective attention.

If you want to be successful in your career or in any aspects of your life, you must learn how draw attention to yourself, in an ethical way, and to use that to your advantage. Those we get promoted faster than their peers would almost always have the attention of their bosses, where they have proven in their abilities and shone louder than their competition and that is why they win. But I want to highlight again that you should do things that help you gain attention ethically.

If you are a business owner, you need to know how to grab the attention of your customers, to be spending more time and money on your products and services. Whether this be done through smart marketing, or word of mouth, you need to draw people's attention to the stuff you are selling. Because even if you have the best product on Earth, it would not be any good if no one is aware of it in the first place.

I challenge each and everyone of you today to find ways that you can draw attention to the areas in your life that feel could use a boost. Come up with solid plans to get more eyeballs looking at you or your products. And i guarantee you that success will come your way a lot sooner.

Chapter 13:
How To Rid Yourself of Distraction

Distraction and disaster sound rather similar.

It is a worldwide disorder that you are probably suffering from.

Distraction is robbing you of precious time during the day.

Distraction is robbing you of time that you should be working on your goals.

If you don't rid yourself of distraction, you are in big trouble.

It is a phenomenon that most employees are only productive 3 out of 8 hours at the office.

If you could half your distractions, you could double your productivity.

How far are you willing to go to combat distraction?

How badly do you want to achieve proper time management?

If you know you only have an hour a day to work, would it help keep you focused?

Always focus on your initial reason for doing work in the first place.

After all that reason is still there until you reach your goal.

Create a schedule for your day to keep you from getting distracted.

Distractions are everywhere.

It pops up on your phone.

It pops up from people wanting to chat at work.
It pops up in the form of personal problems.
Whatever it may be, distractions are abound.

The only cure is clear concentration.
To have clear concentration it must be something you are excited about.
To have clear knowledge that this action will lead you to something exciting.

If you find the work boring, It will be difficult for you to concentrate too long.
Sometimes it takes reassessing your life and admitting your work is boring for you to consider a change in direction.

Your goal will have more than one path.
Some paths boring, some paths dangerous, some paths redundant, and some paths magical.
You may not know better until you try.
After all the journey is everything.

If reaching your goal takes decades of work that makes you miserable, is it really worth it?
The changes to your personality may be irreversible.

Always keep the goal in mind whilst searching for an enjoyable path to attain it.

After all if you are easily distracted from your goal, then do you really want it?

Ask yourself the hard questions.
Is this something you really want? Or is this something society wants for you?

Many people who appear successful to society are secretly miserable.
Make sure you are aware of every little detail of your life.
Sit down and really decide what will make you happy at the end of your life.

What work will you be really happy to do?
What are the causes and people you would be happy to serve?
How much money you want?
What kind of relationships you want?
If you can build a clear vision of this life for you, distractions will become irrelevant.
Irrelevant because nothing will be able to distract you from your perfect vision.

Is what you are doing right now moving you towards that life?
If not stop, and start doing the things what will.
It really is that simple.

Anyone who is distracted for too long from the task in hand has no business doing that task. They should instead be doing something that makes them happy.

We can't be happy all the time otherwise we wouldn't be able to recognize it.
But distraction is a clear indicator you may not be on the right path for you.
Clearly define your path and distraction will be powerless.

Chapter 14:
How Much Is Your Time Really Worth?

What is the biggest mistake we make in life? Perhaps Buddha's most suitable answer was given by "The biggest mistake is you think you have time." While our time in this world is free, it's also priceless. We can neither own it nor keep it, but we can use it and spend it. And once it's all lost, it's inevitable that we will never get it back.

"Your time is limited, so don't waste it living someone else's life." - Steve Jobs. Our time is limited in this world is both good and bad news. The bad news is that time flies and never returns, but the good news is that we're the pilot. The average person lives 78 years on this planet. We spend almost one-third of our lives sleeping; that's approximately 28.3 years from our lives. And still, 30% of us struggle to sleep well. We spend almost 10.5 years of our life working, but over 50% of us want to leave our current jobs. Time is a valuable asset, even more so than money. We can get more money, but we can never get more time.

After all of the years we spend doing chores, shopping, grooming, eating, drinking, TV, and social media, time leaves us with only nine years. Now the question arises, how will we spend that time? Just like we would never waste our money on something gratuitous, why do we waste our time on it? We might think that people are wasting our time when we are the ones permitting them to do that in reality. We sometimes end up losing our most beloved people because we don't value their time. Some of us don't recognize their importance until they're gone.

Every day, from the moment we wake up till the moment we get back to sleep, two voices are battling inside our heads; one wants to uplift us and one that holds us back. And which one will win? The one that we listen to the most. The one that we feed us the most. The one that we amplify. Similarly, it's up to us and our choice how we use that time in our hands. William Shakespeare once said, "Time is prolonged for those who want, very fast for those who are scared, very long for those who are sad, and very short for those who celebrate, but for those who love, time is eternal." We should make the most out of our time and learn its value by carefully analyzing what life teaches us about it.

Chapter 15:
<u>Be Inspired to Create</u>

Some of you will look in the mirror today and think that you are weird. You will see that you are different to other people. That you are quirky or odd. But I want to encourage you. Not only is your uniqueness something that you should embrace but it is perhaps your greatest asset. The wonderful thing about people being different is that they think a little differently, see the world from a slightly different perspective. The combination of the various bits of knowledge that they have fit together in different ways.

When you speak you are most likely not conscious of your accent. Maybe if you live in a foreign country you are hyper aware of it. But how many of you know that your mind has an accent too. It has an accent that is formed from your experiences. Your experiences with pain. Your experiences with joy. Your experiences with success, failure and even your experiences with the everyday mundane. Not only that but the accent of your mind constantly evolves.

Why does that matter?

Because it is that accent which enables you to innovate. When you speak a foreign word, it takes on a new form in your accent – sometimes it may even be a sound that has never been uttered with that tone and inflection. It is completely original not because of the form of the word but because of the accent that informs the way the word comes out.

The same is true of your mind. You can speak the same ideas, study the same fields, even research the exact same thing and still end up with different outcomes. How? Because your outcomes are being informed by your experiences. Your ideas are your present thoughts running rampant through familiar thought patterns. They are tailored towards a particular style. For some of you it is like your mind rolls the r's in your ideas. It adds a certain *je ne sais quoi* to your ideas. To others your accent is thick and mutes the aesthetic nuances of ideas – manifesting in wonders of logic and mechanics.

Whatever it may be, I encourage you to embrace the accent of your mind. Actually, I demand you to. It is time that you stopped denying the world of your contribution to it. It's time that you got inspired to create. It is time that you allowed ideas to implode within the realm of your consciousness and innovations to pour out of it. Whether you find your language in art, dance, engineering, or politics. If you have a niche area of knowledge or see a pattern from a unique combination of information then it is about time you harnessed that and rode the creation train to wherever it may take you. I can promise you that you will never look back. We tend to regret the things we did not do, not the things that we did.

Listen closely and hear the accentuation of your thoughts. Then speak their creative ingenuity into being.

Create something that only you can.

Chapter 16:
When To Listen To That Voice Inside Your Head

Everyday we hear a voice in our head telling us things to us. Whether it be a negative voice telling us not to do something, or a positive one that pushes us to try something new, we sometimes forget when and when not to listen to it.

Today I found myself in that very situation. I found myself walking going about my day when I heard a voice telling me that I should go back to my passion, which was to record music, and simply used my voice as the only tool to make music. I had heard this voice many times before, but i always brushed it away because I thought to myself, no one is going to want to hear me sing. Why should anyone? My voice sucks. It's not as good as other people. No one is going to like it. And I am just going to waste my time. Those negative voices always found a way to beat down my positive one to the point where I just gave up listening to them altogether because I figured that I was never going to act on anything out of my fears to do so anyway.

But something happened today that made me listen. Today I felt like it had a point to make and it was trying to get out. and today those goblin voices that usually tried to kill that positive one was silent. I took that opportunity to head straight down to the nearest electronics store, to buy an expensive mic, and decided that I was going to pursue this venture no matter what. I wanted to do it for myself. I wanted to do it because I didn't want to regret not listening to that inner voice 10-20-30 years down the road. Sure people might still not listen to me sing, but dammit i was going to do it anyway.

It didn't matter to me if only 5 people liked it. It mattered more that I liked it. It mattered more that I overcame myself and finally put music out there that I was proud of.

I bought that mic because I didn't want the excuses in my head to start creeping up on me again. I bought that mic because it gave me no way out. I was already committed. And if I didn't do it I would've just wasted a ton of money. Sometimes in life you have to push yourself and give no reasons to turn back. Because it is always easy just to give up. But when that object is staring at you, sitting and calling out to you, you are going to one to use it.

We all have voices in our heads that tell us to do something crazy but magical in our lives. We shove them aside because we are afraid. We shove them aside because we don't dare to dream. We shove them aside because we think we are not good enough. We fail to realize that we are just one decision away from changing our lives.

Carrie Underwood, for those of you who don't know who she is, she won American Idol in 2005 and became one of the biggest country music superstars in the world. Did you know that she almost didn't make the trip to audition for American Idol because that goblin voice in her head told her it was a stupid idea to go? In that split second decision where she decided to try anyway, it changed her life forever. She changed the music scene forever. It was crazy to think a girl from a small town could win as many Grammys as she did, but she did.

This is the same dilemma you and I face everyday. We fail to realize that everytime we say no to that crazy idea, we are taking one step back in our lives. Soon we become so used to taking these steps back that we end up taking them forever, failing to achieve anything great in the process. Life is simply one giant list of decisions that we make on a daily basis. Any decision that we choose not to take, is a decision that is either missed, or lost.

Start listening to what that voice inside your head has been telling you to do. Has there been something that has been painfully obvious to you? A voice that has been recurring that you've been shoving aside? Take a pen, write that voice down on apiece of paper. Dig into it and start finding out if you should be taking action on it. You never know what that one decision can do for the rest of your life unless you give it a shot.

Chapter 17:
<u>Overcoming the Fear of Failure</u>

Stop it.

Stop whatever you are doing and take a moment to listen because you need to hear this...

Right now I want you to close your eyes and remember a time that you failed. I want you to remember how it made you feel. Remember the pain. Remember the guilt. Dig deep and remember the crushing weight of DISAPPOINTMENT that dragged you down to the depths of hell.

Do you feel it?! DO YOU REMEMBER THAT FEELING?! Good. Now get used to it - because you're gonna feel it again.

I need you to understand that failure is a part of life. In fact it's more than that. It's an essential part of life, of success! You think winners never failed? You think it's just you? Winners have failed more times than losers have ever TRIED!

People who succeed don't stop when they fail. They don't stop at ten, fifty or a hundred failures! They push through. They persevere. It doesn't matter how many times they get knocked down. They get right back up. Again. And again. And again. You know why? They don't fear failure.

Listen closely, because this will change your life. So long as you fear failure, you will never achieve success. You will never reach your dreams. Fearing failure is the only thing stopping you from becoming great. Greatness is a title reserved only for those who are willing to go head to head with failure - for those who face the fear of failure without hesitation! They look failure in the eye and say "I'll be damned if I let YOU sat and in my way!"

When they asked Michael Jordan how many shots he made, you know what he said? He told them they were nothing compared to how many he missed. Michael Jordan became the greatest basketball player of all time because he wasn't afraid to fail! What do you think would have happened if he had given up? If he had been scared to fail. He would never have become the legend that he did. He would have stayed a nobody - just like you.

Did that hurt? How did it make you feel? The pain. The guilt. The disappointment of knowing that so long as you fear failure YOU WILL BE A NOBODY. Your talent, your ability, the greatness within you! They will all die within you. If you aren't ready to accept that, then you need to make a change.

Get up. Get up from wherever you are hiding and face failure one on one. That fear is the only thing standing between you and success. You've got to get it through your head that this is it, the moment of truth. This is the time to decide who you are. Either you are a winner or a loser. If you can't look failure in the eye to achieve your dreams then you will never rise beyond mediocrity. But if you are a winner, now is the time to prove it. Forget mediocrity, you rise to the occasion. Failure is nothing more than one step closer to the greatness you desire. And if you can do that, if you can overcome the fear of failure... you can do anything.

Chapter 18:
How To Deal With Uncertainty?

How many of you are going through life right now but are dealing with a load of uncertainty that is weighing heavily on your mind?

You could be worrying about your career or work related matters: you wonder because the economy is taking a hit, whether you will still have your job tomorrow, whether your business would survive, or even if the economy is good, you are uncertain if you quit the current job you hate whether you are able to find another job in the near future or if you will even be competent in your new profession.

Or you could be worrying about your loved ones, your child who is studying overseas, or your spouse where they are working in the healthcare profession, working in the police or fire department, or even the military, where their lives are put at risk every single day, you worry if there will be one day that you might lose them and they won't come home.

Or you could be uncertain about smaller matters, matters such as if your date went well and if they would give you a call to ask you out again.

Whatever these may be, they all fall under the umbrella of uncertainty.

I would like to share with you uncertainties I faced personally and I would like to provide you with action steps to deal with them.

Recently I had been struggling with many uncertainties in my life. While they might not be your struggles I believe I would be able to provide more value if i shared my own story.

The first uncertainty I had was that I had recently restarted my publishing business after being away from it for a year, I was so afraid of what the market condition was like now, I was afraid of the competition, I was afraid I would fail again. I was afraid I would waste more of my time building up a business only to have it taken away from me.

The second worry I had was that I had also just begun taking my real estate exam to become a licensed realtor. I started having doubts about myself that I would ever become a competent realtor like my peers and I would look like a fool and I would feel disappointed with myself thereafter.

The next uncertainty I had was whether I would get the jobs that I applied for. I had decided to take on a part or full-time position to grow my professional career and I was afraid Whether the hours I spent on job applications would be in vain and that i would get no responses or even worse, rejections.

The final uncertainty was with stocks. Due to the incredible market volatility, I couldn't sleep properly every night because I wasn't sure what was gonna happen tmr. Whether I was gonna lose money while i was asleep.

I went about days with all these negative thoughts looming in my mind. It affected my sleep, my well-being, and my happiness. I started becoming dreary, unhappy, and lifeless. I spent 80% of my waking hours with these fears and doubts, and constantly beating myself up for feeling this way and it only made matters worse.

One day I decided it was enough. I took a deep breath and started collecting myself. I had had enough and I was so done with feeling these uncertainty and feeling sorry for myself.

I made the decision to accept my struggles, that they were a part of life and that there was no point in worrying about it. I decided it that I would just work hard on these areas, keep doing my best, and that whatever outcomes doesn't matter because I've given it my all. And finally I decided to live my day to the fullest and just be grateful that I even get to have the opportunity to pursue these ventures. After going through this process day in and day out, I became more at peace with myself. I started feeling less anxiety and adopted a more optimistic and positive mindset.

Here's what I realized. Uncertainty is born out of fear. This could be fear of losing someone, fear of the unknown, or even fear of failure. I had immense fears of failure that it crippled me to a really low point in my life. And the only way to overcome fear is first to accept that it is normal to be fearful, and then after to not let that fear get in the way of your happiness because life is too short for you to spend in a state of fearfulness. Rather, spend your time feeling grateful for your life and just try your best in everything that you do. Keep working on your dreams as if it were your last day on this earth, keep loving your spouse or child as though it was their last day on this earth, and ask yourself, is this how you would want to spend your time letting fear and uncertainty feed on your happiness? Or would you rather cherish every single moment you have with yourself and your family, and to live life with abundance instead.

This is my challenge to you. Uncertainty can only cripple you if you let it. Focus on your journey, your path, and trust in the process. But most importantly, Trust in yourself, believe in yourself even if no one else will. You owe that much love and compassion to yourself. I know you can do it.

Chapter 19:
The Only Obstacle Is Yourself

Ever wondered why you feel low all the time?
Why it seems like everyone is better than you?
Why everyone excels at something that you wished you were good at too?

I am sure you have wondered about at least one of these at one or another instance in your life.

These questions remain unanswered no matter how hard you try. Until you realize that the only answer that fits the puzzle is that, it is because of you.

All these barriers and limitations are placed upon you not because you are stupid or incapable.
It is merely because you have limiting beliefs about yourself that stop you from achieving your fullest potential.
It is because you are not trying hard enough to make yourself stand apart from everyone else in the world.

If you lag at school, study hard.
If your lag at your job, socialize more.
If you are obese, break a sweat to lose all that fat.

If you lack some technical skill, learn till you beat the very best in that field.

Don't blame others for your failures.
Everyone else starts off with the same resources and expertise as you.
If others can succeed, Why can't you?
Who is stopping you from flying high in victory?
If no one else tells you, let me do the honors; it's you.

You are the biggest cause of everything that is happening in your life right now.
Nothing is good or bad unless you do or don't do something to generate that result.

Make a promise to yourself today that you will achieve something great by the end of this week.
Envision the big picture and start watching yourself get drawn into that picture.

Take baby steps. take a big leap of faith.
Move one foot forward over the other no matter how big or small.
Once you get past the fear of being stuck where you currently are,
life will start opening great doors to your every step forward.

Sometimes we may take a step back.
Sometimes life throws us durians instead of lemons.

As long as you dust yourself off and move again you are never going to lose.

Don't idealize someone if you are not ready to idealize yourself.
To envision yourself charting your own path, in your own unique pair of shoes.

If for whatever reason you don't achieve that something someday, don't beat yourself up for it.
Maybe those shoes weren't the right fit for you.
Try another pair of shoes, and walk down a new path with confidence.

This could be a blessing in disguise for you.
A lesson for you to strive towards something new.
Something better. Something that no one has ever dreamed of or done before.

If along the way some someone comes and tells you to stop, and you stop to hear them say that to you, it wasn't their fault, but yours. Because you were idle enough to be distracted by others to compromise that dream.

Don't lift your head until you have achieved something today. Don't say a word to anyone about your goals.

Spend more and more time to figure out your life. Promise yourself that no one else matters in your life till you have achieved everything and you are left with nothing more to achieve.

I remember the time my father told me to be a better man than him. The time when I fell off my bicycle for the first time. He came to me and said, 'Don't give up now, as you will fall every day, but when you rise you will achieve bigger and better things than you could ever wish'.

My father gave me his hand when I needed it the most and he still does. But when he is gone and there is no one free enough or caring enough left to see me go through all that struggle, then I will be the closest figure to my father to back me up and give me the courage to get up and start again till I succeed in riding the bike of life.

You and I are capable of riding the high tide. Either we ride it all the way to the shore or we drown to never get back up again. It's up to us now what we want to do. It's you who decides what you were and what you can be!

You will regret yourself the most when you finally come to realize that it was 'You' who brought you down. So don't waste yourself and make a vow today, a vow to be the best you can be and the rest will be history.

Chapter 20:
7 Ways To Know If You're A Good Person

This question is something that we wonder from time to time. When we are at our lowest point and we look around, there could be a chance that there may not be that many people in our lives that we can really count on.

We start to wonder how people actually see us. Are we good people? Have we been nice to those around us? Or do we come off as pretentious and hence people tend to stay clear of us for some reason.

There is a dilemma lately about the use of social media and having followers. It seems that people are interested in following your socials, but when it comes to you asking them out or chatting them up, they don't respond or are uninterested to meet up with you.

You then start to wonder if there is something wrong with you. You start to question your morals, your self-worth, and everything about your life. This can quickly spiral out of control and lead to feelings that you are somehow flawed.

Today we're going to help you answer that question: Am I a good person? Here are 7 Ways To Find Out If You Are Indeed One

1. Look At The People Who Have Stuck Around

I think this one is a good place to start for all of us. Instead of wondering if we have gone wrong somewhere, take a look at the friends and family who have stuck around for you over all this time. They are still there for you for a reason. You must have done something right for them not to leave you for other people. Sure some of them may not be as close as they once were, but they are still there. Think about the people who celebrate your birthdays with you, the people who still asks if you want to hang out from time to time, and the people who you can count on in times of emergency. We may not be able to determine if we are good people from this, but we know that at least we are not so far off the rails.

2. Ask Them To Be Honest With You

If you really want to find out if you are a good person, ask your friends directly and honestly, to point out to you areas that they feel you need to work on. Sometimes we cannot see the flaws and the misguided actions that we portray to the world. People may gradually dislike and drift away from us quietly without telling us why. The people who have stuck around know you best, so let them be brutally honest with you. Take what they have to say as constructive criticism, rather than a personal attack on your character. It is better to know in what areas you lack as a person and to work to improve it, than to go through life obliviously and thinking that there is absolutely nothing wrong with you.

3. Think About Why Your Friends May Not Respond To Your Messages

Many a times friendships simply run its natural course. As work, relationships, and family come into the picture, it is inevitable that people drift apart over time. If you decide to hit your friends up and they don't respond, don't take it too personally. It could be that maybe you're just not a vital piece of the puzzle in their lives anymore. If their friendships aren't one that you have been cultivating anyway, you may want to consider removing them completely from your lives. Find new people who will appreciate and love you rather than dwell on the past. There may be nothing wrong with you as a person, it's just the cruel nature of time playing its dirty game.

4. Keeping It Real With Yourself

Do you think that you are a good person? The fact that you are here shows that you may already have an inclination that something may not be quite right with you but you can't quite put a finger on it. Instead of looking for confirmation from external sources, try looking within. Ask yourself the hard questions. Think about every aspect of your life and evaluate yourself. If you have more enemies than friends, maybe there is something you aren't doing quite right that needs some work. Write those possible flaws down and see if you can work through them.

5. Do You Try Your Best To Help Others?

Sometimes we may not be great friends but we may be great at other things, such as being passionate about a cause or helping other people. Maybe friendships aren't a priority for us and hence it is not a good indicator of whether we are good people by looking at the quality of our friendships. If instead we are driven by a cause bigger than ourselves, and we participate through volunteering, events, and donation drives, we can pat ourselves on the back and say that at least we have done something meaningful to better the lives of others. In my opinion you are already a winner.

6. Is Life Always About What You Want?

This one could be a red flag because if we create a life that is only centred around us, we are in danger of being self-obsessive. Having the "Me First" attitude isn't something to be proud of. Life is about give and take, and decisions should be made fairly for all parties involved. If you only want to do things your way, or go to places you want, at the expense of the opinions of others, you are driving people away without realising it. Nobody likes someone who only thinks about themselves. If you catch yourself in this position, it may be time to consider a 180 turn.

7. People Enjoy Being Around You

While this may not be the best indicator that you are a good person, it is still a decent way to tell if you are well-liked and if people enjoy your presence. Generally people are attracted to others who are kind, loyal, trustworthy, and charismatic. If people choose to ask you out, they could find you to be one of those things, which is a good sign that you're not all too bad. Of course you could have ulterior motives for presenting yourself in a well-liked manner, but disingenuity usually gets found out eventually and you very well know if you are being deceitful to others for your own personal gain.

Conclusion

There is no sure-fire way to tell if you are a good person. No one point can be definitive. But you can definitely look at a combination of factors to determine the possibility of that age-old question. The only thing you can do is to constantly work on improving yourself. Invest time and effort into becoming a better person and never stop striving for growth in your character.

Chapter 21:
Do More of What Already Works

In 2004, nine hospitals in Michigan began implementing a new procedure in their intensive care units (I.C.U.). Almost overnight, healthcare professionals were stunned by its success.

Three months after it began, the procedure had cut the infection rate of I.C.U. Patients by sixty-six percent. Within 18 months, this one method had saved 75 million dollars in healthcare expenses. Best of all, this single intervention saved the lives of more than 1,500 people in just a year and a half. The strategy was immediately published in a blockbuster paper for the New England Journal of Medicine.

This medical miracle was also simpler than you could ever imagine. It was a checklist.

This five-step checklist was the simple solution that Michigan hospitals used to save 1,500 lives. Think about that for a moment. There were no technical innovations. There were no pharmaceutical discoveries or cutting-edge procedures. The physicians just stopped skipping steps. They implemented the answers they already had on a more consistent basis.

New Solutions vs. Old Solutions

We tend to undervalue answers that we have already discovered. We underutilize old solutions—even best practices—because they seem like something we have already considered.

Here's the problem: *"Everybody already knows that"* is very different from *"Everybody already does that."* Just because a solution is known doesn't mean it is utilized.

Even more critical, just because a solution is implemented occasionally doesn't mean it is implemented consistently. Every physician knew the five steps on Peter Pronovost's checklist, but very few did all five steps flawlessly each time.

We assume that new solutions are needed to make real progress, but that isn't always the case. This pattern is just as present in our personal lives as it is in corporations and governments. We waste the resources and ideas at our fingertips because they don't seem new and exciting.

There are many examples of behaviors, big and small, that have the opportunity to drive progress in our lives if we just did them with more consistency—flossing every day—never missing workouts. Performing fundamental business tasks each day, not just when you have time—apologizing more often. Writing Thank You notes each week.

Of course, these answers are boring. Mastering the fundamentals isn't sexy, but it works. No matter what task you are working on, a simple checklist of steps you can follow right now—fundamentals that you have known about for years—can immediately yield results if you just practice them more consistently.

Progress often hides behind boring solutions and underused insights. You don't need more information. You don't need a better strategy. You just need to do more of what already works.

Chapter 22:
Becoming High Achievers

By becoming high achievers we become high off life, what better feeling is there than aiming for something you thought was unrealistic and then actually hitting that goal.

What better feeling is there than declaring we will do something against the perceived odds and then actually doing it.

To be a high achiever you must be a believer,

You must believe in yourself and believe that dream is possible for you.

It doesn't matter what anyone else thinks , as long as you believe,

To be a high achiever we must hunger to achieve.

To be an action taker.

Moving forward no matter what.

High achievers do not quit.

Keeping that vision in their minds eye until it becomes reality, no matter what.

Your biggest dream is protected by fear , loss and pain.

We must conquer all 3 of these impostors to walk through the door.

Not many do , most are still fighting fear and if they lose the battle, they quit.

Loss and pain are part of life.

Losses are hard on all of us.

Whether we lose possessions, whether we lose friends, whether we lose our jobs, or whether we lose family members.

Losing doesn't mean you have lost.

Losses are may be a tough pill to swallow, but they are essential because we cannot truly succeed until we fail.

We can't have the perfect relationship if we stay in a toxic one, and we can't have the life we desire until we make room by letting go of the old.

The 3 imposters that cause us so much terror are actually the first signs of our success.

So walk through fear in courage , look at loss as an eventual gain, and know that the pain is part of the game and without it you would be weak.

Becoming a high achiever requires a single minded focus on your goal, full commitment and an unnatural amount of persistence and work.

We must define what high achievement means to us individually, set the bar high and accept nothing less.

The achievement should not be money as money is not our currency but a tool.

The real currency is time and your result is the time you get to experience the world's places and products , so the result should always be that.

The holiday home , the fast car and the lifestyle of being healthy and wealthy, those are merely motivations to work towards. Like Carrots on a stick.

High achievement is individual to all of us, it means different things to each of us,

But if we are going to go for it we might as well go all out for the life we want, should we not?

I don't think we beat the odds of 1 in 400 trillion to be born, just to settle for mediocrity, did we?

Being a high achiever is in your DNA, if you can beat the odds, you can beat anything.

It is all about self-belief and confidence, we must have the confidence to take the action required and often the risk.

Risk is difficult for people and it's a difficult tight rope to walk. The line between risk and recklessness is razor thin.

Taking risks feels unnatural, not surprisingly as we all grew up in a health and safety bubble with all advice pointing towards safe and secure ways. But the reward is often in the risk and sometimes a leap of blind faith is required. This is what stops most of us - the fear of the unknown.

The truth is the path to success is foggy and we can only ever see one step ahead, we have to imagine the result and know it's somewhere down this foggy path and keep moving forward with our new life in mind.

Know that we can make it but be aware that along the path we will be met by fear, loss and pain and the bigger our goal the bigger these monsters will be.

The top achievers financially are fanatical about their work and often work 100+ hours per week.

Some often work day and night until a project is successful.

Being a high achiever requires giving more than what is expected, standing out for the high standard of your work because being known as number 1 in your field will pay you abundantly.

Being an innovator, thinking outside the box for better practices, creating superior products to your competition because quality is more rewarding than quantity.

Maximizing the quality of your products and services to give assurance to your customers that your company is the number 1 choice.

What can we do differently to bring a better result to the table and a better experience for our customers?

We must think about questions like that because change is inevitable and without thinking like that we get left behind, but if we keep asking that, we can successfully ride the wave of change straight to the beach of our desired results.

The route to your success is by making people happy because none of us can do anything alone, we must earn the money and to earn it we must make either our employers or employees and customers happy.

To engage in self-promotion and positive interaction with those around us, we must be polite and positive with everyone, even with our competition.

Because really the only competition is ourselves and that is all we should focus on.

Self-mastery, how can I do better than yesterday?

What can I do different today that will improve my circumstances for tomorrow.

Little changes add up to a big one.

The belief and persistence towards your desired results should be 100%, I will carry on until… is the right attitude.

We must declare to ourselves that we will do this , we don't yet know how but we know that we will.

Because high achievers like yourselves know that to make it you must endure and persist untill you win.

High achievers have an unnatural grit and thick skin , often doing what others won't, putting in the extra hours when others don't.

After you endure loss and conquer pain , the sky is the limit, and high achievers never settle until they are finished.

Chapter 23:
Overcoming Fear and Self-Doubt

The lack of belief most people have is the reason for their failure at even the smallest things in life. The biggest killer of dreams is the lack of belief in ourselves and the doubt of failure.

We all make mistakes. We all have some ghosts of the past that haunt us. We all have something to hide. We all have something that we regret. But what you are today is not the result of your mistakes.

You are here because of your struggles to make those things go away. You are here now with the power and strength to shape your present and your future.

Our mind is designed to take the shape of what we hold long enough inside it. The things we frequently think about ultimately start filling in the spaces within our memory, so we have to be careful. We have to decide whether we want to stay happy or to hold on to the fear we once wanted to get rid of.

The human spirit and human soul are colored by the impressions we ourselves decide to impose.

The reason why we don't want to explore the possibility of what to do is that subconsciously we don't believe that it can happen for us. We don't believe that we deserve it or if it was meant for us.

So here is something I suggest. Ask yourself, how much time in a day do you spend thinking about your dream? How much time do you spend working on your dreams everyday? What books did you read this year? What new skills have you acquired recently? What have you done that makes you worthy of your dream? Nothing?

Then you are on point with your doubt because you don't have anything to show for when the opportunity presents itself.

You don't succeed because you have this latent fear. Fear that makes you think about the consequences of what will happen if you fail even with all the good things on your hand?

I know that feeling but failure is there to teach you one important and maybe the most essential skill life can teach us; Resilience.

You rediscover your life once you have the strength to fight your every fear and every doubt because you have better things on your hand to care for.

You have another dream to pursue. Another horizon awaits you. Another peak to summit. It doesn't matter if you literally have to run to stand still. You got to do what you got to do, no matter the consequences and the sacrifices.

But failing to do what is required of you has no justifiable defense. Not even fear. Because your fears are self-imposed and you already have many wrong things going on for you right now.

Don't let fear be one of them. Because fear is the most subtle and destructive disease So inhale all your positive energies and exhale all your doubts because you certainly are a better person without them.

Chapter 24:
<u>Get in the Water (Stop wasting time)</u>

Stop wasting time.

If you have something to do, then do it. It is literally that simple. Nobody likes something hanging over their head, it is stressful and pressurising and the longer you leave it, the more of a challenge it is going to be. Just get it done.

It's like getting into cold water. You can start by dipping your big toe in, then walking away and reconsidering, before putting all five of them in, maybe if you are feeling frisky you'll put in your whole foot. It is such a waste. You know you are going to get in the water eventually so you might as well dive in. Otherwise, you will spend 80% of your time drawing out an adjustment that could literally take a few seconds. What is the point? Just dive in and get it over with. Does it take a bigger first-off effort, yes. But it saves you so much time and energy afterwards. After the initial shock and a few seconds of feeling like your skin is trying to shrivel up, you are fine.

If we can do it with cold water then we can do it with that email, project or book. You can dive right into all that research you need to do. Yes, it seems overwhelming, and that first leap is going to be full of questions and discomfort. Mid-air you will probably be asking what you got yourself into but the great thing is that you can't stop mid-air. There's no turning around and floating on the air until you reach solid ground again. You are committed now.

The powerful thing is that 90% percent of your problem is inertia. It is that first step. It's sitting down, firing up your laptop and starting to work. It is getting past the idea that you have so much work to do and just focussing on what you can do right now. But when it comes down it you must realise that there is no work around for that. You cannot not do that first step. Even if it is just a passion you know that passion is going to keep burning you up on the inside until you allow it to burst out. There's no getting past the cold water, there is only getting into it. So you might as well jump. If you are trying to write a book, then sit down and just start typing. Even if you are not even typing words, just sit down for 25 minutes and type away at your keyboard. Then, while you are typing you will realise that you are sitting down and pressing the keys anyways so they may as well say something that make sense. I don't care if what you type is cliché because at this point we are not worried about quality. I don't care how good your form is in your butterfly stroke if you are not even in the water. You just need to get started so that you are moving. And once you are moving you can maximise on your momentum.

Chapter 25:
Creating Successful Habits

Successful people have successful habits.

If you're stuck in life, feeling like you're not going anywhere, take a hard look at your habits.

Success is built from our small daily habits accumulated together,

Without these building blocks, you will not get far in life.

Precise time management, attention to detail, these are the traits of all who have made it big.

To change your life, you must literally change your life, the physical actions and the mindset.

Just as with success, the same goes with health.

Do you have the habit of a healthy diet and regular athletic exercises?

Healthy people have healthy habits.

If you are unhappy about your weight and figure, point the finger at your habits once again.

To become healthy, happy and wealthy, we must first become that person in the mind.

Success is all psychological.

Success has nothing to do with circumstances.

Until we have mastered the habits of our thinking we cannot project this success on the world.

We must first decide clearly who we want to be.

We must decide what our values are.

We must decide what we want to achieve.

Then we must discipline ourselves to take control of our destiny.

Once we know who we are and what we want to do,

Behaving as if it were reality becomes easy.

We must start acting the part.

That is the measure of true faith.

We must act as if we have already succeeded.

As the old saying goes: "fake it UNTIL YOU MAKE IT"

Commit yourself with unwavering faith.

Commit yourself with careful and calculated action.

You will learn the rest along the way

Every habit works towards your success or failure,

No matter how big or how small.

The more you change your approach as you fail, the better your odds become.

Your future life will be the result of your actions today.

It will be positive or negative depending on your actions now.

You will attain free-will over your thoughts and actions.

The more you take control, the happier you will be.

Guard your mind from negativity.
Your mind is your sanctuary.
Ignore the scaremongering.
Treat your mind to pure motivation.

We cannot avoid problems.
Problems are a part of life.
Take control of the situation when it arises.
Have a habit of responding with action rather than fear.

Make a habit of noticing everybody and respecting everybody.
Build positive relationships and discover new ideas.
Be strong and courageous, yet gentle and reasonable.
These are the habits of successful leaders.

Be meticulous.
Be precise.
Be focused.

Make your bed in the morning.
Follow the path of drill sergeants in the royal marines and US navy seals.
Simple yet effective,
This one habit will shift your mindset first thing as you greet the new day.

Choose to meditate.

Find a comfortable place to get in touch with your inner-self.
Make it a habit to give yourself clarity of the mind and spirit.
Visualize your goals and make them a reality in your mind.

Choose to work in a state of flow.
Be full immersed in your work rather than be distracted.
To be productive we need to have an incredible habit of staying focused.
It will pay off.
It will pay dividends.
The results will be phenomenal.

Every single thing you choose to make a habit will add up.
No matter how big or how small,
Choose wisely.

Choose the habit of treating others with respect.
Treat the cleaner the same as you would with investors and directors.
Treat the poor the same as you would with the CEO of a multi-national company.
Our habits and attitude towards ourselves and others makes up our character.

Choose a habit of co-operation over competition,
After all the only true competition is with ourselves.
It doesn't matter whether someone is doing better than us as long as we are getting better.

If someone is doing better we should learn from them.
Make it a habit of putting ourselves into someone else's shoes.
We might stand to learn a thing or two.

No habit is too big or too small.
To be happy and successful we must do our best in them all.

Chapter 26:
Focus On The Work You Need To Do Today

Today we're going to talk about the topic focus, and not just that, but to be very precise on exactly what you need to do each and everyday from the very beginning.

It is easy for us to get lost in the sea of things we need to do each day. From work carried over from yesterday, to the commitments that have made for the brand new day, we can forget what our priorities are over time. It is all too easy to get busy and feeling like you're being productive only to come out of it realising that you hadn't really done anything at all. Or rather that you haven't been doing the things that really matter that will move the needle forward for you in life.

When you are unclear about what you need to do, it can be all too easy to focus on the wrong things from the moment you wake up. Maybe you forgot that you need to work on your side business that you hope would one day bring you the time freedom that you crave. Maybe you forgot that you were supposed to study for that real estate exam that is supposed to help you bring some passive income while you work on your day job. Maybe you forgot that you needed to work on yourself, to become a better person so that you can be a better father, mother, parent, lover, spouse, partner, whatever your role may be. It can become all too easy to get busy with chatting with your friends on messaging apps or busy with rearranging your house or tidying up and decluttering, that the day gets away from you in the blink of an eye.

Remember that you only have one life to live and everyday is incredibly precious that should not be wasted. For every minute that you waste, they turn into hour, days, months, and before you know it, years and decades later you haven't even begun on the tasks that truly matter in life.

Before we go on I want you again to think about the areas in your life that you said you wanted to focus on. The really important things. The ones that will change your future for the better and the ones that will bring you to whatever you define as success in life. Only when we know exactly what we want can we carve out a plan of action that will take us there.

These areas that you want to pay attention could be your health for example, and you might want to start by choosing the right foods for your first meal every morning. Another area that you might want to focus on could be fitness. Take that first hour of your day to do some workouts that will improve your metabolism so that in your 50s you might still have a healthy body to enjoy the fruits of your labour. In the area of career and finance, you may want to start applying to jobs that are in line with your purpose, or maybe you might want to keep researching on ways to make more money to support you and your family. If the area you want to focus on is family, maybe the first thing you want to do instead is to spend some quality time with them. If your goal is to develop a strong and lasting bond with your wife and kids, you might want to consider carving out a certain amount of time to be with them so that you don't go by years later and realise you were never really present for your family at all. Work and money can be secondary when we realize that love is what really matters. And if your focus is your current job, stop wasting time and start cracking on that project asap. If you feel like you need to work on yourself, you might consider spending an hour every morning reading a self-help book that hopefully helps you grow your personality, or maybe watch a YouTube video like this one that teaches you how to be a better person.

The idea here is that there is no one template for everybody. You are your own person and your area of focus is unique. Only you know where you need to work on and only you know the plan of action you need to take if you want to see true and lasting change.

So I challenge each and everyone of you to clearly define the areas of your life that needs your most attention. Drill down on it each and every day. Don't stop putting the pedal on the gas in these areas. Occasionally it's okay to wander off course but always find your way back on the horse. 90% of your time should be spent on these areas with total focus. Don't let distraction and passiveness rob you of your time. Also choose to spend time on learning and growing yourself each day and the benefits will be immense.

Chapter 27:

It's Okay To Feel Uncertain

We are surrounded by a world that has endless possibilities. A world where no two incidents can predict the other. A realm where we are a slave to the unpredictable future and its repercussions.

Everyone has things weighing on their mind. Some of us know it and some of us keep carrying these weights unknowingly.

The uncertainty of life is the best gift that you never wanted. But when you come to realize the opportunities that lie at every uneven corner are worth living for.

Life changes fast, sometimes in our favor and sometimes not much. But life always has a way to balance things out. We only need to find the right approach to make things easier for us and the ones around us.

Everyone gets tested once in a while, but we need to find ways to cope with life when things get messy.

The worst thing the uncertainty of life can produce is the fear in your heart. The fear to never know what to expect next. But you can never let fear rule you.

To worry about the future ahead of us is pointless. So change the question from 'What if?' to 'What will I do if.'

If you already have this question popping up in your brain, this means that you are already getting the steam off.

You don't need to fear the uncertain because you can never wreck your life in any such direction from where there is no way back.

The uncertainty of life is always a transformation period to make you realize your true path. These uncertainties make you realize the faults you might have in your approach to things.

You don't need to worry about anything unpredictable and unexpected because not everything is out of your control every time. Things might not happen in a way you anticipated but that doesn't mean you cannot be prepared for it.

There are a lot of things that are in your control and you are well researched and well equipped to go around events. So use your experience to do the damage control.

Let's say you have a pandemic at your hand which you couldn't possibly predict, but that doesn't mean you cannot do anything to work on its effects. You can raise funds for the affected population. You can try to find new ways to minimize unemployment. You can find alternate ways to keep the economy running and so on.

Deal with your emotions as you cannot get carried away with such events being driven by your feelings.

Don't avoid your responsibilities and don't delay anything. You have to fulfill every task expected of you because you were destined to do it. The results are not predetermined on a slate but you can always hope for the best be the best version of yourself no matter how bad things get.

Life provides us with endless possibilities because when nothing is certain, anything is possible. So be your own limit.

Chapter 28:
When It's Okay to Do Nothing

Today I'm going to talk about the topic of when it is okay to do nothing. We're going to be really specific with this one, and that is talking about relaxation and switching off for a while if we feel like life just seems a little too stressful or hard to take.

For many of us who are leading busy lives, life can seem like one big endless to-do list. We attract problems everyday - whether it be from our jobs, our relationships, or children, our parents, our friends, our hobbies, there just doesn't seem like a time when we can just simply do nothing. We are constantly told to keep busy with our lives, to always be doing something, to always be productive, that we forget that sometimes doing nothing may be the best thing once in a while.

As life gets more complicated, so do our problems and responsibilities. From managing a family, paying our bills, being on time with our taxes, expenses, moving houses, changing jobs, we never run out of things to fill our time with. We expand our resources with time and energy day in and day out, never resting, and it takes a huge toll on our bodies physically, mentally, emotionally, and spiritually.

When we operate on such a high level every single day, sometimes even on auto-pilot due to the routine nature of things, we might end up losing sight of who we are and why we are placed on this Earth. We may start to forget why we are doing what we are doing and we simply get lost in the ocean of tasks that need to be completed.

Many of us think that travel is the best time to recharge and relax - but for many of us who plan elaborate trips, travel can sometimes be as exhausting as going to work although with a different agenda. With the limited time we have on our travel and leaves that we are allowed to take, we jam pack our schedule that requires detailed planning and execution. Rushing from place to place to check off landmarks of interests can sometimes be a chore in itself. If we are not careful, even travel can drain us the same way. So what should we do then?

How about nothing?

How about absolutely nothing.

Doing nothing might sound curious to many of you. "What do you mean do nothing?" Some of you might say. It is exactly what it says.

When we have nothing on our agenda, nothing to plan for and nothing to deal with, we find ourselves in a space of our own. A space where we can reflect on the things that are happening in our lives. A space where we can look inwards to check on our current state and feelings. To get in touch with ourselves to see the areas where we might want to improve on. And to be reminded of the direction that we are headed.

You can do nothing by simply finding a quiet place in your house or elsewhere, where you decide to give however long you need to recharge holistically. To make "doing nothing" successful, you have to set yourself up for success. Decide that you will switch off all electronic devices - to purge yourself of technology, of reminders, of deadlines, of your bosses and colleagues, and to find your inner quiet.

If you find sitting quietly and being by yourself can be too daunting of a task, consider finding a guided meditation guide or some soothing music where you can just simply lie and rest uninterrupted. If sleep is what you need in that moment, take a nap. If ideas flash before you, acknowledge them, write them down, your call. Listen to your body and respond to it.

When you practice doing nothing consistently, you will feel that life starts to slow down a little bit more. You start to breathe a little slower and life becomes slightly more manageable when you learn how to take care of yourself.

Instead of only looking forward to holidays and trips to recharge, learn to schedule doing nothing routinely in your calender. Having the ability and power to choose as and when you need to relax and give full and total attention to yourself is as important as the attention and time you give to those around you. Only when you can take care of yourself first can you also take care of others with the same capacity.

So I challenge each and every one of you to put yourself first by making the decision to do nothing. That it is perfectly okay to switch off the crazy life around you for a moment. You can always come back to it once you're fully recharged and ready to rumble again.

Chapter 29:

Be Motivated by Challenge

You have an easy life and a continuous stream of income, you are lucky! You have everything you and your children need, you are lucky! You have your whole future planned ahead of you and nothing seems to go in the other direction yet, you are lucky!

But how far do you think this can go? What surety can you give yourself that all will go well from the start to the very end?

Life will always have a hurdle, a hardship, a challenge, right there when you feel most satisfied. What will you do then?

Will you give up and look for an escape? Will you seek guidance? Or will you just give up and go down a dark place because you never thought something like this could happen to you?

Life is full of endless possibilities and an endless parade of challenges that make life no walk in the park.

You are different from any other human being in at least one attribute. But your life isn't much different than most people's. You may be less fortunate or you may be the luckiest, but you must not back down when life strikes you.

This world is a cruel place and a harsh terrain. But that doesn't mean you should give up whenever you get hit in the back. That doesn't mean you don't catch what the world throws at you.

Do you know what you should do? Look around and observe for examples. Examples of people who have had the same experiences as you had and what good or bad things did they do? You will find people on both extremes.

You will find people who didn't have the courage or guts to stand up to the challenge and people who didn't have the time to give up but to keep pushing harder and harder, just to get better at what they failed the last time.

The challenges of life can never cross your limits because the limits of a human being are practically infinite. But what feels like a heavy load, is just a shadow of your inner fear dictating you to give up.

But you can't give up, right? Because you already have what you need to overcome this challenge too. You just haven't looked into your backpack of skills yet!

If you are struggling at college, go out there and prove everyone in their wrong. Try to get better grades by putting in more hours little by little.

If people take you as a non-social person, try to talk to at least one new person each day.

If you aren't getting good at a sport, get tutorials and try to replicate the professionals step by step and put in all your effort and time if you truly care for the challenge at hand.

The motivation you need is in the challenge itself. You just need to realize the true gains you want from each stone in your path and you will find treasures under every stone.

Chapter 30:
Don't Fear Judgement

People often seem to get caught up in certain areas of their lives where they have a lot to offer but don't actually have the guts to be transparent about it. Let me make some sense.

We all have this ability to get distracted by things that have very little to do with our actions. But have a lot to do with what others will say about us.

You go through a rough patch in life and then you find the balance. We have things that have been going on in our lives from the beginning, but we still feel doubts about it.

The doubt is natural. But if the doubts are a result of the presence of other people around you, then you have a problem at your hand. This problem is the fear of judgment that everyone imposes on us in their own unique ways.

Humans have a tendency to get out of their ways and try certain things that aren't always normal. They may be normal for some, but for most people out there, it's just another eccentric doing something strange.

So what? What is so bad about being a little different? What is wrong with thinking a little out of the box? Why should your approach be bad if someone doesn't approve of it?

These questions should not make you feel confused. Rather should help you get a much clearer idea of what you want. These questions and their answers can help you find the right motivation. The motivation to do your thing no matter what the others around you say or see.

You are the best judge of your deeds. Because no one else saw your intentions when you started. No one else saw the circumstances that led you to these actions. No other person was in your head looking at and feeling those incidents that carved your present state. But you were always there and always will be.

No one cares what you are up to until you get to the stage of being noticeable. People pass judgments because now you have made it into some sort of limelight. It may be your workplace, your college, or even a party where most people are stoned.

But think about it, what harm can you get with a couple of remarks about your outfit or an achievement?

The words that strike your ears and make you feel incompetent or stupid are just the insecurities of the people around you. The glare of shaming or mockery is only the reflection of the feeling that they don't have what you have.

So be who you are, and say what you want, and do what you feel. Because the people who mind don't matter. But the people who matter would never mind.

Come to terms with yourself and be confident with what you want to do or are currently up to.

No one would understand your reasons and no one is meant to. But they can make a judgment when you are finally on that rostrum. Then you'd have the power to shut anyone at any time.

Chapter 31: Discovering Your Strengths and Weaknesses

Today we're going to talk about a very simple yet important topic that hopefully brings about some self discovery about who you really are. By the end of this video i wish to help you find out what areas you are weak at so that maybe you could work on those, and what your strengths are so that you can play to them and lean into them more for greater results in your career and life in general.

We should all learn to accept our flaws as much as we embrace our strengths. And we have to remember that each of us are unique and we excel in different areas. Some of us are more artistic, some visionary, some analytical, some hardworking, some lazy, what matters is that we make these qualities work for us in our own special way.

Let's start by identifying your weaknesses. For those of you that have watched enough of my videos, you would know that i encourage all of you to take a pen to write things down. So lets go through this exercise real quick. Think of a few things that people have told you that you needed to work on, be it from your Teachers, your friends, your family, or whoever it may be.

How many of these weaknesses would you rate as significantly important that it would affect your life in a drastic way if you did not rectify it? I want you to put them at the top of your list. Next spend some time to reflect and look in the mirror. Be honest with yourself and identify the areas about yourself that you know needs some work.

Now I want you to take some time to identity your strengths. Repeat the process from above, what are the things people have told you about yourself that highlighted certain qualities about you? Whether that you're very outgoing, friendly, a great singer, a good team player, very diligent. I want you to write as many of these down as you can. No matter how big or small these strengths are, I want you to write down as many as you can.

Now I want you to also place your 3 biggest strengths at the top of the list. As I believe these are the qualities that best represent who you are as a person.

Now that you've got these 2 lists. I want you to compare them. Which list is longer? the one with strengths or weaknesses? If you have more weaknesses, that's okay, it just means that there is more room for improvement. If you have more strengths, thats good.

What we are going to do with this list now is to now make it a mission to improve our weaknesses and play heavily into our strengths for the foreseeable future. You see, our strengths are strengths for a reason, we are simply naturally good at it. Whether it be through genetics, or our personalities, or the way we have been influenced by the world. We should all try to showcase our strengths as much as we can. It is hard for me to say exactly what that is, but I believe that you will know how you maximise the use of your talent. Whether it be serving others, performing for others, or even doing specific focused tasks. Simply do more of it. Put yourself in more situations where you can practice these strengths. And keep building on it. It will take little effort but yield tremendous results.

As for your weaknesses, I want you to spend some time on the top 3 that you have listed so far. As these could be the areas that have been holding you back the most. Making improvements in these areas could be the breakthrough that you need to become a much better person and could see you achieving a greater level success than if you had just left them alone.

I challenge each and everyone of you to continually play to your strengths, sharpening them until they are sharp as a knife, while working on smoothening the rough edges of your weaknesses. So that they may balance out your best qualities.

Chapter 32:

Don't Be Demotivated By Fear

What are you doing right now? What ambitions do you have for the morning to come? What doubts you have in mind? What is stopping you right now?

You have doubts about anything because you want to be cautious. You are hesitant because you have your gut telling you to think again. The reality is you are afraid and you don't know it. Or maybe you do know it but you keep ignoring your weakness.

That weakness you keep ignoring is your fear. Fear starts with a seed but if left alone can manifest deeper roots and can have a devastating impact on one's personality.

Fear is the biggest enemy of commitment. Fear kills productivity. Fear eats creativity. Fear crushes motivation.

People keep fears as if they are being smart about unexpected outcomes. You don't need to stay afraid of things to abstain from them. The only thing you need to fear is the 'Fear' itself.

When you were a child, your parents motivated you and gave you the confidence to get over most of your fears. But now you would be considered stupid and childish if you seek a mentor. You what do you do?

The answer is simple. You have yourself to try out things that make you take a step back. Because fear is self-imposed. You made yourself prone to such feelings and you can make them go away as well.

Fear can make you second guess your own abilities.

We are way behind our goals because subconsciously we have thought of the failure that can happen. The fear of our dreams shattering overtakes the ambition and happiness when you finally get to the scale. This overburdening feeling of fear keeps us sitting in our seats and stops us from trying out new things. This fear makes us believe that we don't deserve what we have dreamt of.

So I have a question for you! What have you done in the last week, or month or even a year to overcome only the smallest phobia?

If you haven't, it is possible that you won't leave what you have right now and never go for anything more than you can own. This reason is that fear makes you remain content with whatever nature and God have bestowed upon you on time after time. But you won't get up and try to work new things for bigger and better blessings that hard work and some gutsy calls have to offer.

If you can't give up the feeling of harm that might come if you finally decide to indulge in those reluctant goals, take a different approach then. Think of it as what can you be on that other side of the river? What colors does the other side of the canvas have? What laughs can you have if you made that one joke? What gains you can have if you increased just one pound?

If you try to make your fears a medium of self-analysis, maybe you start to gain the motivation that faded quickly with every second you spent in front of that source of fear. Then you might start to see a whole new image of your personality and this might be the person you always wish you could be!

Chapter 33:
Deal With Your Fears Now

Fear is a strange thing.

Most of our fears are phantoms that never actually appear or become real,

Yet it holds such power over us that it stops us from making steps forward in our lives.

It is important to deal with fear as it not only holds you back but also keeps you caged in irrational limitations.

Your life is formed by what you think.

It is important not to dwell or worry about anything negative.

Don't sweat the small stuff, and it's all small stuff (Richard Carlson).

It's a good attitude to have when avoiding fear.

Fear can be used as a motivator for yourself.

If you're in your 30s, you will be in your 80s in 50 years, then it will be too late.

And that doesn't mean you will even have 50 years. Anything could happen.

But let's say you do, that's 50 years to make it and enjoy it.

But to enjoy it while you are still likely to be healthy, you have a maximum of 15 years to make it - minus sleep and living you are down to 3 years.

If however you are in your 40s, you better get a move on quickly.

Does that fear not dwarf any possible fears you may have about taking action now?
Dealing with other fears becomes easy when the ticking clock is staring you in the face.
Most other fears are often irrational.

We are only born with two fears, the fear of falling and the fear of load noises.
The rest have been forced on us by environment or made up in our own minds.
The biggest percentage of fear never actually happens.

To overcome fear we must stare it in the face and walk through it knowing our success is at the other side.
Fear is a dream killer and often stops people from even trying.
Whenever you feel fear and think of quitting, imagine behind you is the ultimate fear of the clock ticking away your life.

If you stop you lose and the clock is a bigger monster than any fear.
If you let anything stop you the clock will catch you.

So stop letting these small phantoms prevent you from living,
They are stealing your seconds, minutes, hours , days and weeks.
If you carry on being scared, they will take your months, years and decades.

Before you know it they have stolen your life.

You are stronger than fear but you must display true strength that fear will be scared.
It will retreat from your path forever if you move in force towards it because fear is fear and by definition is scared.

We as humans are the scariest monsters on planet Earth.
So we should have nothing to fear
Fear tries to stop us from doing our life's work and that is unacceptable.
We must view life's fears as the imposters they are, mere illusions in our mind trying to control us.

We are in control here.
We have the free will to do it anyway despite fear.
Take control and fear will wither and disappear as if it was never here.
The control was always yours you just let fear steer you off your path.

Fear of failure, fear of success, fear of what people will think.
All irrational illusions.
All that matters is what you believe.
If your belief and faith in yourself is strong , fear will be no match for your will.

Les Brown describes fear as false evidence appearing real.
I've never seen a description so accurate.

Whenever fear rears its ugly head, just say to yourself this is false evidence appearing real.

Overcoming fear takes courage and strength in one's self.
We must develop more persistence than the resistance we will face when pursuing our dreams.
If we do not develop a thick skin and unwavering persistence we will be beaten by fear, loss and pain.

Our why must be so important that these imposters become small in comparison.
Because after all the life we want to live does dwarf any fears or set back that might be on the path.
Fear is insignificant.
Fear is just one thing of many we must beat into the ground to prove our worth.
Just another test that we must pass to gain our success.

Because success isn't your right,
You must fight
With all your grit and might
Make it through the night and shine your massive light on the world.
And show everyone you are a star.

Chapter 34:
Never Giving Up

Today I'm going to talk about a topic that I feel very inspired to share. In recent times, never giving up has helped me to push through the initial failures that I had experienced when it came to my career which I later found traction in. I hope that the story today will inspire you also do the same.

It Is all too easy for us to give up when the going gets tough. Starting something new is always much easier but sticking through it and grinding through all the problems that you will most certainly face, is the greater challenge on the road to success that many of us are not willing to put ourselves through.

In recent years, I have had many occasions that it was my persistence that actually yielded the fruits of my labour 2-3 years after I had begun the journey. Success was not found immediately.

A few years ago, I began my online career to make money and I found a new business that I was interested in. I invested time and money into it and found some success in the beginning. I gave up all prior aspirations to pursue a traditional career to embark on this journey and I had nothing to lose.

However after 2 years pouring my heart and soul in this venture, I faced a tough reality when something happened to my business and I lost everything. I lost my sole stream of income and I felt absolutely lost, not to mention crushed that all my time had literally gone up in smoke. I started to doubt myself and question why I even bothered embarking on this path in the first place. I really did not know what to do and had no

Plan B. I spent the next few months wandering about trying to figure out what's next. At one point I did feel like giving up and going back to finding a regular job despite knowing that that is something I really did not want to do.

After months of exploring, I decided that I would give my first venture another go. I created a new account and began the journey again, from scratch. I faced many obstacles that were not there before and the struggle was terribly real. I felt pressure from myself to make it work because I felt that there was nothing I was really good at. I needed to prove to myself that I wasn't a failure and that fire lit up inside me to be successful at it at all cost.

To put it simply, eventually my persistence did pay off and I managed to build back some of the income stream that I had lost with new strategies that I had employed. What I only realised much later was that it was actually my experience having been in the business for two years prior that helped me navigate this new strategy much quicker. Everything was done at lightning speed despite the obstacles and I was astounded by the pace in which it picked up. It was in that moment that I understood the principle of never giving up. Because if I had, I would have literally flushed away all the time and energy I had invested earlier in the business down the toilet. It was my attitude of never giving up, and learning from my mistakes that got me through the second time around.

Another story that I want to share about never giving up is something much simpler, and it had to Do with something that happened around the house. In a random event, somehow my door got jammed by an appliance around the house. And no matter how hard I tried to push it simply wouldn't budge. After cracking my head for hours, together with my parents, we still couldn't figure out how to get the door to open no matter how many things we tried. At one point my dad decided that the only way was to break down the door. However the persistence in me didn't want to give up. I found a strategy that could possibly work, involving a knife, and long story short I managed to get the door to open with a great deal of strength. In that moment I felt like the king of the world. Never giving up and persisting felt like the greatest feeling on Earth. And it got me fired up to want to apply this same persistence to all aspects of my life.

It was with these joint experiences along with many others that gave me the conviction that solidified the principle that I have been hearing from gurus every single day about never giving up. That only when you had given up have you truly failed. And I believe every single one of those words today.

So I challenge each and everyone of you today to try this out for yourself. To go back to something you have decided that you had called quits on and to give it one more try. Use your expertise, use your experience, learn from your mistakes of what went wrong before, modify the new plan, and try again. You might be surprised at the outcome. Never ever give up because it's never really over until you have decided to quit.

Chapter 35:
Keep Moving When Things Get Hard

Keep to your goals by putting problems into perspective.
In times of difficulty, most give up.
Don't be like those people.

Difficulties are there to challenge us.
Difficulties are there to help us think outside the box.

Seek to change as you seek success.
Things never really stay the same.
Paths are never that straight.
You always come to a fork in the road.

Think of this new life and realise that thoughts will change how you act.
To have of a better life you must first consider losing this one you have now.

To achieve an extreme desired change you lose everything in the process.
It can be a tough pill to swallow.
It can be hard to see the silver lining.

But if you can keep moving towards what you have in mind,
sooner or later the new life will start to take shape.

First you must be unwavering in your faith.

It will get hard before it gets easy.
You must endure the winter to see the spring and summer.
You must weather the storm to see the sunshine.

Hard times come to all those who seek success.
Your courage will be tested.
Your endurance and persistence will be tested.
No one is exempt from this price.

You will find that nearly all your life's problems come from fear, loss, and pain,
but they are not as powerful as they appear.
They are no match for you if you believe that.
They are illusions.
Illusions because they are only real in our minds if we allow them to fester.

Most of your perceived problems never actually happened.
Most of your fears were phantoms of the mind.
Be prepared to lose it all if you desire a new life.

You must push through the pain to receive the gain.
In times of pain and struggle, you will grow.
In times of uncertainty, your bravery will shine through.
If you persist, you will make it through any problem.

You will become successful.

You must defeat the 3 phantoms to reach the promised land of health, happiness and wealth.

Self-mastery is not a battle with yourself.

Self-mastery is letting your inner-self take control.

The more you listen to your gut feeling the better your choices.

Your inner voice knows far more than your brain can tell you.

Problems arise because you have not taken action.

Force that change upon yourself.

You are like a shark.

You will die if you stop moving forward.

You will die if you accept defeat.

You must move forward like a shark.

No matter what,

Just keep swimming.

No matter what,

Get to your desired location

Get tough with yourself.

The outcome hangs in the balance.

Trust your inner compass to guide you.

Help who you can along the way.

Your thoughts will become reality good or bad.

Remain focus on the good despite the bad.

Lasting success is waiting for you.

YOU WILL MAKE IT as long as YOU DON'T QUIT!

Persistence is key.

Persist in getting what you want.

Persist in fighting for the job you desire.

Never give up even if you get rejected 100 times over.

Persistence always pays off.

You will be given your chance to shine if you keep at it.

Life will throw you curveballs.

As long as you are moving forward, you can still change direction.

Keep the dream in mind as you navigate through this uncharted territory.

No matter what,

Belief in yourself and your vision.

Keep trying to find the best people for your organisation and look after them like family.

One action can change your whole situation.

One action can change your entire life.

You will overcome the obstacles if you keep going and keep believing.

Nothing is more powerful than a made-up mind.

Chapter 36:
How To Succeed In Life

"You can't climb the ladder of success with your hands in your pocket."

Every day that you're living, make a habit of making the most out of it. Make a habit of winning today. Don't dwell on the past, don't worry about the future. You just have to make sure that you're winning today. Move a little forward every day; take a little step every day. And when you're giving your fruitful efforts, you're making sure you're achieving your day, then you start to built confidence within yourselves. Confidence is when you close your eyes at night and see a vision, a dream, a goal, and you believe that you're going to achieve it. When you're doing things, when you're productive the whole day, then that long journey will become short in a matter of time.

Make yourself a power list for each day. Take a sheet of paper, write Monday on top of it and then write five critical, productive, actionable tasks that you're going to do that day. After doing the task, cross it off. Repeat the process every day of every week of every month till you get closer to achieving your goals, your dreams. It doesn't matter if you're doing the same tasks every day or how minor or major they are; what matters is that it's creating momentum in things that you've believed you couldn't do. And as soon as the momentum gets completed, you start to believe that you can do something. You eventually stop writing your tasks down because now they've become your new habits. You need a reminder for them. You don't need to cross them off because you're going to do them. The power list helps you win the day. You're stepping out of your comfort zone, doing something that looks uncomfortable for starters, but while doing this, even for a year, you will see yourself standing five years from where you're standing today.

Decide, commit, act, succeed, repeat. If you want to be an inspiration to others, a motivator to others, impact others somehow, you have to self-evaluate certain perceptions and think that'll help you change the way you see yourself and the world. Perseverance, hard-working, and consistency would be the keywords if one were to achieve success in life. You just have to keep yourself focused on your ultimate goal. You will fall a hundred times. There's always stumbling on the way. But if you have the skill, the power, the instinct to get yourself back up every time you fall, and to dig yourself out of the whole, then no one can stop you. You have to control the situation, Don't ever let the situation control you. You're living life exactly as it should be. If you don't like what you're living in, then consider changing the aspects. The person you are right now versus the person you want to be in the future, there's only a fine line between the two that you have to come face-to-face with.

Your creativity is at most powerful the moment you open your eyes and start your day. That's when you get the opportunity to steer your emotions and thoughts in the direction that you want them to go, not the other way around. Every failure is a step closer to success. We won't succeed on the first try, and we will never have it perfect by trying it only once. But we can master the art of not giving up. We dare to take risks. If we never fail, we never get the chance of getting something we never had. We can never taste the fruits of success without falling. The difference between successful people and those who aren't successful is the point of giving up.

Success isn't about perfection. Instead, it's about getting out of bed each day, clearing the dust off you, and thinking like a champion, a winner, going on about your day, being productive, and making the most out of it. Remember that the mind controls your body; your body doesn't hold your mind. You have to make yourself mentally tough to overcome the fears and challenges that come in the way of your goals. As soon as you get up in the morning, start thinking about anything or anyone that you're grateful for. Your focus should be on making yourself feel good and confident enough to get yourself through the day.

The negative emotions that we experience, like pain or rejection, or frustration, cannot always make our lives miserable. Instead, we can consider them as our most incredible friends that'll drive us to success. When people succeed, they tend to party. When they fail, they tend to ponder. And the pondering helps us get the most victories in our lives. You're here, into another day, still breathing fine, that means you got another chance, to better yourself, to be able to right your wrongs. Everyone has a more significant potential than the roles they put themselves in.

Trust yourself always. Trust your instinct—no matter what or how anyone thinks. You're perfectly capable of doing things your way. Even if they go wrong, you always learn something from them. Don't ever listen to the naysayers. You've probably heard a million times that you can't do this and you can't do that, or it's never even been done before. So what? So what if no one has ever done it before. That's more of the reason for you to do it since you'll become the first person to do it. Change that 'You can't' into 'Yes, I definitely can.' Muhammad Ali, one of the greatest boxers to walk on the face of this planet, was once asked, 'how many sit-ups do you do?' to which he replied, 'I don't count my sit-ups. I only start counting when it starts hurting. When I feel pain, that's when I start counting because that's when it really counts.' So we get a wonderful lesson to work tirelessly and shamelessly if we were to achieve our dreams. Dr. Arnold Schwarzenegger beautifully summed up life's successes in 6 simple rules; Trust yourself, Break some rules, Don't be afraid to fail, Ignore the naysayers, Work like hell, And give something back.

Chapter 37:
Being Mentally Strong

Have you ever wondered why your performance in practice versus an actual test is like night and day? Or how you are able to perform so well in a mock situation but just crumble when it comes game time?

It all boils down to our mental strength.

The greatest players in sports all have one thing in common, incredibly strong beliefs in themselves that they can win no matter how difficult the circumstance. Where rivals that have the same playing ability may challenge them, they will always prevail because they know their self-worth and they never once doubt that they will lose even when facing immense external or internal pressure.

Most of us are used to facing pressure from external sources. Whether it be from people around us, online haters, or whoever they may be, that can take a toll on our ability to perform. But the greatest threat is not from those areas… it is from within. The voices in our head telling us that we are not going to win this match, that we are not going to well in this performance, that we should just give up because we are already losing by that much.

It is only when we can crush these voices that we can truly outperform our wildest abilities. Mental strength is something that we can all acquire. We just have to find a way to block out all the negativity and replace them with voices that are encouraging. to believe in ourselves that we can and will overcome any situation that life throws at us.

The next time you notice that doubts start creeping in, you need to snap yourself out of it as quickly as you can, 5 4 3 2 1. Focus on the next point, focus on the next game, focus on the next speech. Don't give yourself the time to think about what went wrong the last time. You are only as good as your present performance, not your past.

I believe that you will achieve wonderful things in life you are able to crush those negative thoughts and enhance your mental strength.

CPSIA information can be obtained
at www.ICGtesting.com
Printed in the USA
LVHW082033170422
716440LV00015B/1286

9 789814 952767